CW01213122

Original title:
The Spectrum of Support

Copyright © 2024 Swan Charm
All rights reserved.

Author: Kätriin Kaldaru
ISBN HARDBACK: 978-9916-86-641-2
ISBN PAPERBACK: 978-9916-86-642-9
ISBN EBOOK: 978-9916-86-643-6

Lighthouses in the Fog

In the mist, they stand so tall,
Guiding ships through tempest's call.
Their beams cut through the dampened night,
Beacons of hope, casting light.

Pillars of Strength

Through storms and trials, they remain,
Unyielding hearts that bear the strain.
With hands held high, they lift us near,
Roots run deep, banishing fear.

Encounters in Empathy

A shared glance, a silent nod,
In this moment, we find the God.
Hearts entwined, we break the mold,
In tiny acts, compassion's bold.

A Mosaic of Aid

Pieces scattered, colors bright,
Together forming a radiant sight.
From many hands, we build the whole,
In unity, we find our soul.

A Quilt of Kindness

Soft threads weave in harmony,
Stitches bind hearts, made to share.
Every patch tells a story,
Of love sewn with tender care.

Bright colors blend with purpose,
Each square whispers hope and grace.
Together, we find our solace,
In this warm, embracing space.

Hands that give, hands that hold,
Embrace the fragile, wounded souls.
A tapestry of tales retold,
Wrapped in kindness, love consoles.

Every fold a gentle touch,
In the fabric, peace is found.
A quilt that mends and heals so much,
In its warmth, we all surround.

So let us gather, let us make,
More quilts of kindness, hand in hand.
With every stitch, joy we create,
A world united, brightly planned.

Guiding Stars

In the dark of night they shine,
Beacons bright with steady light.
They lead the lost, a simple sign,
Chasing away the endless fright.

Each twinkle tells a secret dream,
An endless dance in cosmic time.
Through shadows, hope begins to beam,
A celestial rhythm, a silent rhyme.

When paths feel hidden, lost from sight,
Their glow ignites the courage deep.
With every glance, they spark our flight,
To leap from doubt and break the sleep.

So gaze above, let wonder grow,
As twinkling guides embrace your heart.
In every star, let love bestow,
A promise that we'll never part.

With guiding stars, we find our way,
Upon this journey, bold yet bright.
No matter night, or break of day,
They'll shine for us, our endless light.

The Dance of Dependability

In moments crisp and shadows long,
With steady steps, we find our place.
Together we hum a loyal song,
In this dance, we share our grace.

Each move a promise, strong, sincere,
Echoes of trust in every turn.
Dependability draws us near,
In gentle rhythms, hearts will learn.

Through storms we stand, hand in hand,
A circle woven, firm and true.
In every sway, we understand,
The strength in me lies also in you.

So let us twirl through life's embrace,
With laughter light upon our feet.
In this shared dance, we find our space,
A tapestry, so pure and sweet.

The dance goes on, forever bright,
A trusted tune we'll always share.
With every beat, we find our light,
In dependability, love declares.

The Quilt of Togetherness

Stitches bind our hearts with thread,
In colors bright, love's fabric spread.
Each patch a dream, a story shared,
In warmth of closeness, we are ensnared.

Together we weave in joy and strife,
Our hands create a tapestry of life.
With every tear, we mend and sew,
In the quilt of love, together we grow.

A design of laughter, memories dear,
In the quiet moments, we hold near.
With every stitch, a bond is formed,
In this patchwork warmth, we are all warmed.

Through storms and sun, we stand as one,
Each square a journey, a race well run.
Together we rise, we fall, we stand,
In the quilt of togetherness, hand in hand.

In every corner, a bright surprise,
Reflections of truth in our loving eyes.
We gather close, our hearts aligned,
In this woven circle, our souls entwined.

Hands Held High

Together we rise, our spirits soar,
With hands held high, we seek for more.
In unity, we find our might,
With every heartbeat, we ignite.

The world may tremble, shadows loom,
But with joined hands, we push the gloom.
A circle of strength, a bond so true,
With hands held high, we will break through.

Through trials faced, and battles won,
Together, our fight has just begun.
So side by side, we face the night,
With hope in hearts, hands held tight.

Each voice a note, in harmony,
Together we sing, in symphony.
With love as our guide, we light the way,
With hands held high, come what may.

In every struggle, we shall find,
With hands held high, we're intertwined.
Together as one, we will prevail,
With strength in unity, we shall not fail.

Trails of Tenderness

In gentle whispers, paths unfold,
Through trails of tenderness, we behold.
With every step, a bond we chase,
In nature's arms, we find our place.

The rustling leaves, a soothing sound,
In shared silence, love is found.
Together we wander, hearts aglow,
On trails of tenderness, we freely flow.

With every turn, a glimpse of grace,
In laughter's echo, we embrace.
As sunbeams dance upon our skin,
On trails of tenderness, we begin.

Through valleys deep and mountains high,
Together we reach, we touch the sky.
In shared moments, our spirits lift,
On trails of tenderness, a precious gift.

With hands entwined, we forge ahead,
In every journey, love is spread.
Through every challenge, we will go,
On trails of tenderness, love will grow.

A Symphony of Allies

In this grand orchestra, we play our part,
A symphony of allies, united heart.
With each note struck, our spirits dance,
Together we march, given the chance.

The drums of courage beat so strong,
In harmony, we know we belong.
With strings of passion, we sing as one,
A symphony of allies, we've just begun.

The winds of change, they guide our song,
Through every struggle, we all stay strong.
In the chorus of voices, we find our way,
A symphony of allies, day by day.

In every challenge, we will rise,
With melodies woven, we lift the skies.
Together we stand, through thick and thin,
A symphony of allies, we all win.

As the final note rings clear and bright,
Our bond remains, a radiant light.
In this vast world, we find our tune,
A symphony of allies, forever in bloom.

Beyond the Shadows

In the twilight's gentle embrace,
We wander where whispers trace.
Dreams linger, secrets unfold,
Stories of bravery, softly told.

Through the darkness, light shall break,
A glimmer of hope, for courage's sake.
Hidden paths, where fears dissolve,
In the heart's refuge, we evolve.

Each step echoes, a chant of old,
Guiding souls, fearless and bold.
Beyond the shadows, a dawn ignites,
Awakening strength, unseen lights.

Through the trials, we find our way,
Hand in hand, come what may.
Trust the journey, the map we chart,
Beyond the shadows, a brand new start.

Luminescent Bonds

Between our hearts, a thread of gold,
Woven bright, a story told.
In laughter shared, in silence too,
The warmth of us in all we do.

Stars may fade, yet we shall shine,
Through storms of life, your hand in mine.
In moments cherished, love is found,
Connected deeply, forever bound.

Though distances stretch, and tides may shift,
Our spirits dance, a timeless gift.
With every heartbeat, a promise renews,
In the light of trust, our bond imbues.

Time may fly, but here we stand,
Embracing truths, side by side we band.
In the glow of hope, we light the way,
Luminescent bonds, come what may.

Unseen Foundations

Beneath the surface, roots entwine,
An unseen strength, pure and fine.
Each heartbeat echoes through the years,
Building dreams while facing fears.

In quiet moments, wisdom stirs,
The gentle whispers, history blurs.
Through trials faced, we rise anew,
Foundations strong, in all we do.

Layer by layer, we forge our path,
With each storm weathered, we find our wrath.
In silence, strength, our spirits soar,
Unseen foundations, forevermore.

Together we stand, unyielding and tall,
Embracing the rise, and preventing the fall.
In every struggle, our resolve is shown,
Unseen foundations, a love we've grown.

Resonance of Resilience

Like the waves crash upon the shore,
Resilience sings, forevermore.
In every setback, a lesson learned,
A spirit unbroken, brightly burned.

Through shadows cast and trials faced,
In courage found, our fears replaced.
With voices strong, we rise and bend,
In the dance of strength, we find a friend.

Echoes of hope, in hearts reside,
Through tempests faced, we turn the tide.
In unity's strength, we stand as one,
Resonance of resilience, battles won.

With every heartbeat, we forge ahead,
No longer bound by words unsaid.
In the tapestry of life, we weave,
The resonance of strength, we believe.

Serenade of Solidarity

In the quiet of the night,
Voices rise in gentle might.
Hand in hand, we stand as one,
Together under the warm sun.

Through the storm and through the strife,
Weaving dreams that bring us life.
Hearts entwined, our spirits soar,
In solidarity, we are more.

With laughter soft and tears that blend,
Each moment shared, we will defend.
In the echo of our song,
We find the place where we belong.

Side by side, we take a stand,
Every heartbeat, every hand.
United strength in strength we'll find,
A serenade for all mankind.

So let us sing, let voices blend,
In the harmony of friend to friend.
For in the echoes, truth shall dwell,
In solidarity, we wear our shell.

Harmonizing Hearts

In a world that's often loud,
We find solace in the crowd.
Melodies of love arise,
As we seek our common ties.

Notes of laughter fill the air,
In every heart, there's room to share.
Together we can learn to weave,
A tapestry that we believe.

Hands reaching out, a warm embrace,
In the dance of time and space.
With every step, a bond we make,
Harmonizing hearts that won't forsake.

In the silence, we still speak,
In every smile, in every peek.
Unified in this sweet art,
Our rhythm flows, we play our part.

So let us sing, let voices ring,
In joyful hearts, our spirits cling.
Together we can touch the skies,
Harmonizing hearts, our love implies.

The Gift of Togetherness

In simple moments, time will show,
The beauty found in hearts that glow.
In laughter's echo and warmth's embrace,
Togetherness is our saving grace.

Through shadows cast and trials faced,
We gather strength and never haste.
In every joy and every tear,
A gift unfolds when you are near.

With whispered hopes and dreams we share,
The bond we build is ever rare.
In silence strong, in voices clear,
The gift of love, we hold it dear.

With every story told tonight,
We shine our truths, igniting light.
Together we can break the mold,
In unity, our hearts are bold.

So let us cherish every day,
In togetherness, come what may.
A vibrant tapestry we weave,
In the gift of love, we all believe.

Nurturing Spirits

In gentle winds, our spirits rise,
Roots entwined beneath the skies.
With every laugh, a seed we sow,
Nurturing love that starts to grow.

Amidst the trials that life unfolds,
We find the warmth in hearts of gold.
In every touch, a spark ignites,
Nurturing souls in tranquil nights.

With kindness shared, our spirits blend,
Every hand extended is a friend.
In the garden of our trust, we see,
The beauty that comes from you and me.

Through whispered words and tender care,
We build a home that we both share.
In every moment, love's embrace,
Nurturing spirits, a sacred space.

So let us tend to this bouquet,
With each new dawn, love finds its way.
Together, we shall ever shine,
In nurturing hearts, our lives align.

Radiant Affirmations

I rise with the sun, bright and new,
Every breath whispers dreams to pursue.
With each step, I find my grace,
In this journey, I embrace my place.

Clouds may gather, yet I stand tall,
With inner light, I won't let it fall.
Today I choose joy, love, and peace,
In my heart, these treasures increase.

The whispers of doubt, I choose to ignore,
My spirit ignites, and I yearn for more.
Every challenge is a chance to grow,
In the garden of life, my colors glow.

Through storms and shadows, I stay aligned,
With courage and hope, I boldly unwind.
Gratitude blooms, an endless song,
In this symphony, I boldly belong.

So here I stand, radiant and free,
The universe unfolds magic for me.
With affirmations, I light the day,
In this wondrous dance, I find my way.

Love's Architecture

In every beam, in every wall,
Love builds a space that won't let us fall.
Foundations strong, with laughter laid,
In this structure, memories cascade.

Windows wide to let fears out,
They echo love; that's what it's about.
Rooms filled with warmth, hearts intertwine,
In every corner, your hand in mine.

Bridges span over trials we've faced,
Each step forward, our bond embraced.
The roof protects, holds dreams above,
In our home, we flourish through love.

Under one sky, we share our dreams,
With time and patience, love always beams.
Together we stand, builders in sight,
Crafting our future, shining so bright.

Each blueprint sketched with hopes unfurled,
In love's architecture, our hearts are swirled.
With every laugh, every tear that flows,
A testament to the life that grows.

Pebbles of Positivity

Small pebbles form a tranquil stream,
Each one a thought, a brightening dream.
I toss them in, watching them dance,
Each ripple spreads, creating a chance.

In quiet moments, they gently shine,
Reminding me that I'm truly divine.
I gather them close, one by one,
In this collection, I find the fun.

Each pebble whispers of hope and grace,
A token of joy in this vast space.
With open heart, I embrace the light,
In this journey, I shine so bright.

I build a path with every thought,
Each stone a lesson that life has taught.
Together they guide my steps ahead,
In the garden of dreams, I'm beautifully led.

So here's to the pebbles, so small yet grand,
With positivity, I take a stand.
In every stone, the magic unfolds,
A treasure of light in my heart it holds.

Unbreakable Chains

From heart to heart, a bond is found,
Together we forge, in love, we're bound.
Through life's storms, we wear our links,
In the silence, it's love that thinks.

Every struggle, like metal in flame,
Strengthens the chain, ignites our name.
With every challenge, we rise anew,
In this unity, our spirits grew.

The weight we carry is shared with grace,
In our eyes, hope finds its place.
With words unspoken and hands held tight,
We navigate dark, finding our light.

In laughter and tears, our ties expand,
The metal forged, forever will stand.
Together we'll face the unknown road,
In this union, we lighten the load.

So let the world test our mighty link,
For in love's chains, we'll never sink.
With strong connection, we claim our reign,
Boundless and free, unbreakable chain.

Waves of Warmth

Gentle tides kiss the shore,
Bringing whispers from afar.
Hues of dawn in soft embrace,
Each wave tells a tale of grace.

Sunlight dances on the sea,
Warming hearts, setting them free.
In the rhythm, we belong,
A melody, sweet and strong.

Embrace the warmth, let it flow,
In tidal currents, love will grow.
With every crest, we stand in awe,
Nature's cradle, tender, raw.

Embracing the Colors of Care

In the garden, blooms arise,
Colors bright, beneath the skies.
Each petal whispers, soft and clear,
The beauty wrapped within our care.

Painted sunsets, warm and bold,
Stories of love, quietly told.
In every shade, connection's found,
Hearts united, joy unbound.

Brush the world with kindness bright,
Let compassion be our light.
With open arms, we share the hue,
Embracing colors tried and true.

Threads of Togetherness

Woven tightly, hand in hand,
Threads of love across the land.
Each moment shared, a stitch we make,
In the fabric of life, hearts awake.

With laughter's echo, joy transforms,
In unity, our spirit warms.
Each thread a story, bold and bright,
Connected souls in day and night.

Together we weave, strong and wise,
In every bond, endless ties.
Through trials faced, we stand as one,
In the tapestry of joy, we run.

Beneath the Umbrella of Kindness

Rain may fall, but we will stand,
Under kindness, hand in hand.
Sheltered safe from storms that roar,
Compassion thrives, forevermore.

Each droplet brings a chance to share,
A gentle touch, a loving care.
Beneath this canopy, take flight,
In every heart, the spark of light.

With open hearts, we greet the day,
Finding warmth in every ray.
Together strong, we face the rain,
Beneath this umbrella, love will reign.

Dances of Unity

In fields of green, we gather near,
With hands entwined, we share no fear.
Each step we take, a bond we weave,
Together, in this dance, we believe.

A circle forms, we spin around,
With laughter bright, a joyful sound.
Our hearts aligned, like stars that shine,
In unity's embrace, we intertwine.

Through valleys wide, our spirits soar,
In harmony, we seek for more.
Each movement tells a tale so true,
A rhythm of love, both old and new.

With whispered dreams, we light the way,
In every heartbeat, hope will stay.
Together we rise, through night and day,
In this dance of life, we'll never sway.

Shelter from the Storm

When winds howl loud and shadows creep,
Your warmth is where my heart can leap.
A sturdy roof, a love profound,
In your embrace, I'm safe and sound.

Through pouring rain, we stand as one,
With every drop, a battle won.
Your laughter breaks the darkest night,
A beacon strong, a guiding light.

When thunder roars and fears arise,
We'll find our peace beneath the skies.
With whispered hopes, our fears will fade,
In this stronghold, our love is made.

Together here, we brave the storm,
With open hearts, a bond so warm.
Through every tempest, we'll remain,
In shelter found, we'll dance through pain.

Voices in the Echo

In valleys deep, where whispers fade,
Echoes linger, secrets laid.
Each voice a story, soft and clear,
Together we rise, embracing fear.

With courage held, we speak our truth,
In every word, the spark of youth.
From shadows cast, we find our song,
In harmonies, we all belong.

The echoes call from times long past,
With every note, our souls hold fast.
In unity, our dreams take flight,
Voices woven, day and night.

For every heart that dares to sing,
The echoes join, a love to bring.
In every pulse, in every beat,
We'll chase the echoes, bittersweet.

Lanterns in the Night

Beneath the stars, our lanterns glow,
In darkness deep, their light will show.
Each flicker speaks of hope and dreams,
As shadows dance in silver beams.

Through winding paths, we find our way,
With every step, we choose to stay.
As lanterns sway in gentle breeze,
Our hearts align, our souls at ease.

The night may whisper fears unknown,
But in this light, we're not alone.
Together here, we share a spark,
Guiding us through the deepest dark.

With every flicker, love will thrive,
In glowing warmth, we feel alive.
Through trials faced, we'll hold on tight,
In unity, our lanterns bright.

A Canvas of Compassion

In every brushstroke, love takes flight,
Colors blend, painting the night.
Understanding wraps us tight,
A canvas of compassion shines so bright.

Hands outstretched in gentle grace,
Healing hearts, a warm embrace.
Together we find our place,
In the beauty of the human race.

Whispers echo in quiet rooms,
Kindness blossoms, dispelling glooms.
Every soul, a flower blooms,
In the garden where compassion looms.

Laughter dances on the breeze,
Moments shared bring inner peace.
With every puzzle piece,
Our compassion swells and never cease.

Through trials faced, together we stand,
Painting hope with a steady hand.
In this world, so vast and grand,
A canvas of compassion, through love, we've planned.

Threads of Togetherness

In the fabric of life, we weave,
Threads of love, together we believe.
Each moment shared, a gift received,
In this tapestry, we're never deceived.

Stitch by stitch, we find our way,
In laughter and tears, we choose to stay.
Bound by whispers, in night and day,
Threads of togetherness never fray.

Different colors, yet strong and true,
In every heart, a vibrant hue.
Together, we form a beautiful view,
In this journey, there's room for you.

When shadows loom and fears arise,
We hold each other, no goodbyes.
Through unity, our spirits rise,
Threads of togetherness, love never dies.

In every heartbeat, we find our song,
Together we stand, where we belong.
In this dance of life, we are strong,
Threads of togetherness, forever lifelong.

Embracing the Rainbow

After the storm, the colors appear,
A spectrum bright, so vivid and clear.
Hand in hand, we conquer fear,
Embracing the rainbow, we draw near.

Each hue tells a story bold,
A tapestry of dreams unfold.
In unity, our hearts turn gold,
Embracing the rainbow, with love retold.

Red for passion, blue for peace,
Green for growth that will never cease.
Together we find, our joys increase,
Embracing the rainbow, a sweet release.

Through every shadow and every light,
We paint the world, a wondrous sight.
In acceptance, we unite,
Embracing the rainbow, our future bright.

With open arms, we celebrate,
All walks of life, we cultivate.
In love's embrace, it's never too late,
Embracing the rainbow, together we create.

Shades of Solace

In the quiet, listen close,
Among the stillness, we can chose.
Finding peace in simple prose,
Shades of solace, where love grows.

Beneath the stars, hearts intertwine,
In whispered dreams, the world aligns.
In the shadows, hope brightly shines,
Shades of solace, a bond divine.

The softness of a gentle breeze,
Brings comfort, sets the spirit at ease.
In shared moments, we find our keys,
Shades of solace, the heart agrees.

With every tear, we cleanse the soul,
In vulnerable times, we become whole.
Together we find, we've reached our goal,
Shades of solace, a cherished role.

In laughter's echo, we discover light,
In every struggle, we gain insight.
Through the journey, side by side we fight,
Shades of solace, our endless flight.

Daring to be There

In shadows cast by doubt, we stand,
With hearts aflame, we walk the land.
Braving storms with steadfast trust,
In every moment, we must adjust.

Our laughter echoes in the night,
With every step, we find the light.
Together we shall forge the way,
In dreams alive, we boldly sway.

Through tangled paths, we carve anew,
With courage deep, we push on through.
Each voice a thread, a vibrant hue,
In unity, we are the glue.

The unknown beckons, bold and bright,
A promise wraps the world in light.
With hands held high, we dare to see,
The beauty in our synergy.

With hopeful hearts, we take our part,
The call to be is the bravest art.
In every heartbeat, bold and rare,
We find our strength, daring to be there.

Caresses of Community

In the circle of warm embrace,
Laughter dances, a joyful space.
Voices harmonize in the air,
Together, we craft a love affair.

Sharing burdens, lifting the weight,
In every moment, we celebrate fate.
The ties we weave are strong and true,
In every heart, a home renew.

Whispers of kindness fill the days,
In laughter and tears, we lay our ways.
Hand in hand, we walk this ground,
In the sanctuary, love is found.

Woven stories, each thread a part,
A tapestry stitched by every heart.
In the caresses of this embrace,
We find our sanctuary, our place.

Through every challenge, we unite,
Together we rise, our spirits bright.
In the caresses of community,
We find our strength and unity.

Hearts Intertwined

In threads of gold, our souls align,
With every breath, our hearts entwine.
Through trials faced and laughter shared,
In silent moments, we have bared.

As seasons change, our roots grow deep,
In whispered dreams, our thoughts we keep.
Through storms and sun, we ever strive,
In every heartbeat, we feel alive.

Two paths converged, a journey bold,
In stories woven, love's tale told.
With open arms, we greet the night,
Together, we shine, a dazzling light.

The magic flows in simple grace,
In every glance, a soft embrace.
With hands together, we design,
A world embraced, our hearts entwined.

In quietude, our spirits blend,
Two souls as one, a timeless trend.
In every dream, we dare to find,
The beauty of our hearts entwined.

Guardians of the Glimmers

In twilight hues, our voices rise,
Guardians stand 'neath starlit skies.
With watchful eyes and steady hands,
We hold the light where hope expands.

Through darkest nights, we shine our flame,
In every heart, we know their name.
A flicker here, a spark held tight,
Together we dance in the falling light.

In gentle whispers, we share our dreams,
Each glimmer grows in endless streams.
We lift each soul, we fan the fire,
In every heartbeat, we inspire.

For every dawn that breaks anew,
We vow to stand, to see it through.
In bonds unbroken, we shall thrive,
Guardians fierce, we keep hope alive.

With every dawn, our spirits soar,
Together, we'll open every door.
With love ablaze, shine bright and clear,
Guardians of glimmers, we hold dear.

Kites in the Wind

Up in the sky, they dance and fly,
Colors bright against the blue,
Childish laughter fills the air,
Hope takes flight, dreams feel anew.

Tails trailing softly in the breeze,
Twisting, twirling, wild and free,
Each pull a flicker of delight,
Threads of joy binding you and me.

We chase them high, with hearts so light,
Through fields of green, we run and play,
With every gust, our spirits soar,
Whispering secrets of the day.

When the sun sets, and they descend,
We gather close, share tales of fun,
In memories stitched like pastel threads,
Kites in the wind, never done.

Echoing Support

In quiet moments, voices ring,
A gentle nudge, a steady hand,
Through troubled times, we hold the line,
Each word a lifeline, softly planned.

Like echoes bouncing off the walls,
Support surrounds, both near and far,
In times of need, we find our strength,
Together shining, like a star.

Through laughter shared, or tears we shed,
In solidarity, we find our way,
The bonds we forge, a mighty force,
Resilience grows with each new day.

A chorus built on trust and care,
In unity, our hearts will thrive,
Empowered by the love we share,
With every heartbeat, we survive.

Rivers of Trust

Clear waters flow, their paths unwind,
Tracing journeys, deep and vast,
In winding trails, the truths we find,
Our spirits tethered to the past.

Rippling softly, whispers drift,
Through stones and roots, they intertwine,
In the current's dance, we give,
Each moment builds, a grand design.

Trust like a river, steady and wide,
Reflecting dreams that shape our fate,
With open hearts, we cannot hide,
Together rowing, never late.

As streams converge, creating depth,
We find our way through storms and sun,
In flowing hope, we take our steps,
Forever bound, and still as one.

A Symphony of Care

In gentle notes, compassion sings,
A melody that warms the heart,
Through every rise, and every fall,
In perfect harmony, we start.

Each voice a thread in woven sound,
A tapestry of love and grace,
As we embrace, our souls unbound,
A symphony, a sacred space.

With every chord, we lend our strength,
In unison, we rise and sway,
Together through the longest length,
Our spirits dance in bright array.

In whispers soft and laughter loud,
We share the notes of joy and care,
A timeless gift, we wrap around,
Creating beauty everywhere.

Pillars of Strength

In shadows cast by doubt, we stand,
Together forged by heart and hand.
With whispers loud, we lift our gaze,
Each step we take, a new embrace.

Amidst the storms, we find our way,
With courage bright, we won't dismay.
Through trials faced, we find our light,
Pillars rise, unwavering might.

The weight of burdens shared anew,
In unity, we break on through.
Through every fall, we learn to rise,
In strength we find our truest ties.

Together we weave a tapestry,
Of dreams and hopes, a legacy.
With every thread, our story grows,
Through every trial, love only shows.

With roots that dig into the earth,
We celebrate our strength and worth.
In harmony, we stand so tall,
Pillars of strength, we will not fall.

Umbrellas of Understanding

When raindrops fall, we gather near,
With open hearts, we share our fears.
One umbrella, many souls,
Beneath its shade, our love consoles.

In quiet moments, we find grace,
Through different paths, we seek one place.
Each story shared builds bridges strong,
In understanding, we all belong.

Amidst the chaos, we take a breath,
With empathy, we conquer death.
The colors of our hearts align,
With open minds, our souls entwine.

As storms may rage, we hold our ground,
In silence deep, our truths are found.
Umbrellas lifted, shelter shared,
In unity, we show we cared.

Together we face what life may send,
In understanding, we will mend.
With hearts as vast as the endless skies,
We'll shield each other, wise and wise.

The Journey Together

With every step, a path unfolds,
Stories written, hearts of gold.
Hand in hand, we choose to share,
A journey rich, a bond so rare.

Through winding roads and fields of green,
We cherish moments, sights unseen.
The laughter echoes, the tears may flow,
Together we rise, together we grow.

The stars above, they guide our way,
In darkest nights, they light the day.
With every mile, our spirits soar,
The journey thrives, forevermore.

We learn and teach, we rise and fall,
In love's embrace, we give our all.
No matter the distance, near or far,
In every heartbeat, we are the star.

Our journey, dear, is never done,
With every sunrise, we are one.
Through every chapter, hand in hand,
The journey together, forever planned.

Strength in Diversity

Like colors in a vibrant scene,
In differences, our hearts convene.
With open minds, we learn and grow,
In diversity, our spirits glow.

Through varied voices, we find our song,
In every note, we all belong.
From distant lands, we share a dream,
Together as one, we flow like stream.

Each culture rich, a tale to tell,
Embracing all, we rise and swell.
From every peak and valley low,
Strength in diversity is how we grow.

With hands entwined, we stand as one,
In unity, our work is done.
For every heartbeat that we share,
Strength in diversity, love is rare.

Together we weave a world so bright,
In every shade, we share our light.
With hearts combined, we lift the rest,
In diversity, we are truly blessed.

The Tide of Togetherness

In the ebb and flow, we unite,
With hands held steadfast, hearts ignite.
The waves of change may crash and roar,
Together we stand, forevermore.

Through storms we weather, side by side,
In the warmth of trust, we take pride.
Our bonds, like anchors, hold us fast,
In the sea of life, our love will last.

As tides may rise, or gently recede,
In each other's strength, we plant a seed.
The ocean whispers, a soft embrace,
In the tide of togetherness, we find our place.

With every wave, we learn and grow,
Through laughter and tears, a steady flow.
In the dance of life, we share the song,
In the tide of togetherness, we all belong.

As day turns to night, we shine like stars,
In the vast expanse, no distance mars.
Together we sail, through calm and strife,
In the tide of togetherness, we find our life.

Mirrors of Motivation

In every glance, reflections gleam,
The spark of hope, a vibrant dream.
Within our eyes, a story told,
Of courage, strength, and hearts of gold.

Each challenge met, a chance to rise,
In mirrored strength, we touch the skies.
Together we fight, our dreams align,
In the mirrors of motivation, we brightly shine.

With words of wisdom, we lift each other,
In every heartbeat, we find a brother.
Through trials faced, we grow and learn,
In the mirrors of motivation, we brightly burn.

Finding light in shadows cast,
In unity, our spirits vast.
With every step, we push the pace,
In the mirrors of motivation, we find our place.

Through whispered doubts, we brave the storm,
With every word, we keep each warm.
Unity fuels the fire within,
In the mirrors of motivation, we all win.

The Heart's Palette

In strokes of love, the heart creates,
Colors of joy, the soul elates.
With every beat, a canvas wide,
In the heart's palette, hopes abide.

Shades of laughter, hues of pain,
Layered stories, a sweet refrain.
In every moment, we paint our fate,
With the heart's palette, we celebrate.

Whispers of kindness, splashes of grace,
In the vibrant chaos, we find our space.
With courage bold, and dreams in sight,
In the heart's palette, we chase the light.

In the silence, a brushstroke flows,
In gentle strokes, the spirit glows.
Creating visions, both deep and bright,
In the heart's palette, love takes flight.

With every heartbeat, our masterpiece grows,
Tales of passion, in color chose.
In life's gallery, a stunning show,
In the heart's palette, our souls will glow.

Wings of Support

In moments heavy, I spread my wings,
To lift you up when sorrow stings.
Together we soar, through clouds of gray,
On the wings of support, we find our way.

When shadows linger and dreams feel lost,
I'll be your shelter, no matter the cost.
In the stormy skies, we navigate,
On the wings of support, we elevate.

Your burdens shared, a gentle grace,
In trust we build, our sacred space.
With every heartbeat, we grow more strong,
On the wings of support, we belong.

Through trials faced, we rise anew,
In unity forged, our spirits true.
Together we dream, together we strive,
On the wings of support, we thrive.

With every challenge, a shade of light,
In friendship's bond, we take flight.
A journey shared, a beautiful art,
On the wings of support, we'll never part.

A Garden of Givers

In a garden where kindness blooms,
Each flower whispers of shared rooms.
Hands that cultivate dreams anew,
Nurturing hope, caring hearts true.

Beneath the sun, joy freely springs,
Feeding the soul with the love it brings.
Roots entwined, we grow as one,
Harvesting light, shining like the sun.

Petals dance in the gentle breeze,
Echoes of laughter filter through trees.
In this haven, we blossom and thrive,
A testament to how we survive.

Seasons change, but hearts remain,
Through rain or shine, through joy or pain.
Together we weather every storm,
Finding strength in each other's warmth.

As dawn breaks with colors so bright,
We stand united, ready to fight.
In this garden, the givers align,
A tapestry woven, eternally fine.

Navigating Through Hues

In twilight's glow, we find our way,
Colors blending, night's gentle sway.
Shadows stretch, as stars ignite,
Guiding us softly through the night.

Violet skies in dreams unfold,
Whispers of secrets, stories told.
Crimson blooms in passionate hearts,
Each moment cherished, a work of art.

Waves of blue crash on the shore,
Whispering tales of what's in store.
In this spectrum, we sail along,
Finding our voice, a vibrant song.

Golden sunlight paints the dawn,
Colors collide; night is withdrawn.
With every hue, a step we take,
Navigating through, no fear to break.

As daylight fades, new shades appear,
Every challenge met without fear.
In life's palette, we paint anew,
A masterpiece crafted by me and you.

Reflections of Resilience

In mirrors of time, we see our scars,
Each line a story, like distant stars.
With courage found in the dark of night,
We rise again, embracing the light.

Storms may rage, and winds may howl,
Yet deep inside, there's no need to cowl.
Strength in our core, with each battle won,
Resilience blooms like the morning sun.

Through trials faced, a path we create,
Building bridges, defying fate.
In shadows cast, we shed our fears,
Transforming pain into strength, not tears.

Echoes of hope reverberate strong,
In the symphony of life, we belong.
With every setback, we choose to soar,
Each challenge faced, we grow ever more.

Reflections tell of a journey vast,
In the tapestry woven, our hearts are cast.
Together we stand, fierce and true,
A testament to what we can do.

Folds of Friendship

In folds of laughter, memories share,
Moments woven, beyond compare.
In quiet corners, our secrets kept,
Promises made, in joy we leapt.

Through valleys low and peaks so high,
Hand in hand, we reach for the sky.
Each stumble met with a guiding light,
In the heart's embrace, hope takes flight.

With every season, bonds intertwine,
Like threads of silver, they brightly shine.
Through storms we weather, through fire we grow,
A steadfast love, ever aglow.

In soft whispers, we find our peace,
In each other's arms, our worries cease.
Through every chapter, we choose to write,
A novel of friendship, pure and bright.

So here's to the journeys, long and sweet,
To every heartbeat, to every greet.
In folds of friendship, we find our place,
A treasure of time, in life's warm embrace.

The Colors of Connection

In the spectrum of our dreams,
We paint with vibrant schemes.
Every hue a story told,
In warm sunlight, not so cold.

Threads of laughter, bonds we weave,
In every glance, we dare believe.
Colors blend, a beautiful sight,
United hearts in pure delight.

From the river to the trees,
Nature whispers through the breeze.
In every shade, a link so strong,
Together, we create our song.

Brushstrokes form a tapestry,
While we dance in harmony.
With openness, we share our pain,
And in sharing, joy we gain.

So let our colors paint the sky,
In unity, we will always fly.
For in each hue, we find our place,
Together, we embrace this space.

Heartbeats in Harmony

In the quiet of the night,
Two hearts offer soft light.
Rhythms sync in a gentle sway,
Guiding dreams along the way.

Echoes dance through the air,
With whispers of love to share.
In every pulse, we find our song,
Where two souls forever belong.

Breath by breath, we draw so close,
In the warmth, we feel engrossed.
Together, we chase the stars,
Navigating life's sweet memoirs.

Moments flutter like a bird,
In silence, every touch is heard.
With each heartbeat, we explore,
An endless love that we adore.

Side by side through fate's embrace,
We journey with a steady pace.
In harmony, our spirits soar,
Two hearts, forever wanting more.

Whispered Encouragements

In shadows deep, a voice will rise,
With gentle words that touch the skies.
Every whisper, soft and clear,
Encouragement, a friend so near.

Through trials faced and battles won,
We lift each other, one by one.
In the struggle, hope is found,
With every word, we stand our ground.

When doubts creep in and spirits fall,
A warm embrace, we heed the call.
In shared strength, a bond is sewn,
A tapestry of dreams we've grown.

With every challenge, we will climb,
In unity, we heal with time.
Through whispered truths, our hearts will mend,
Together, we can always transcend.

So let us share these sounds of grace,
In affirmations, we find our place.
With whispered love in every breath,
We'll nurture life, defy the death.

Voices of Unity

In the chorus of our days,
Together we find our ways.
Voices blend, a symphony,
Creating bonds of harmony.

With every note, we lift the tides,
In the strength of love, we confide.
From silence springs a vibrant sound,
In unity, our hopes abound.

As one we rise, as one we stand,
In a world that meets us hand in hand.
Echoes of dreams we share tonight,
In our hearts, a guiding light.

Through trials faced and hearts laid bare,
Our voices rise in fervent prayer.
For in this union, we are strong,
Together, we will right the wrong.

So let us join in joyous song,
With open hearts, our spirits throng.
In every voice, a truth to see,
Together, we create our harmony.

Currents of Connection

In the quiet of the night, we find,
Threads of fate gently entwined.
Hearts that beat in unison,
A dance of souls, forever one.

Rivers flow with whispered dreams,
Carrying stories, or so it seems.
Each wave a bond, a tale to share,
Bridges built in the open air.

Through the struggles, through the pain,
We rise together, like the rain.
Drops that merge into a stream,
Creating a journey, a shared dream.

With each smile that lights the way,
Connections grow, come what may.
In laughter's echo, we reside,
Unified by love, our guide.

As currents shift and tides may change,
We hold each other, fierce and strange.
In every heartbeat, every glance,
We find our strength, we choose to dance.

Voices in the Wind

Listen close, the whispers call,
Through the trees, they gently fall.
Echoes of laughter, soft and sweet,
Nature's rhythm, our hearts' beat.

In the stillness, stories soar,
Carried on winds to distant shores.
Each sigh a secret, old and wise,
As stars awaken in the skies.

The breeze shares tales of love and loss,
Of bridges crossed and burdens tossed.
With every gust, we start anew,
Join the dance, me and you.

Through the valleys, across the plains,
The wind remembers joyful chains.
It sings of hope, it whispers dreams,
Binding hearts in silver seams.

So let us roam where voices blend,
In harmony, as currents send.
For in the wind, we find our way,
Together, come what may.

The Embrace of Friendship

In laughter's light, our spirits soar,
Together always, forevermore.
Through storms we stand, side by side,
In the embrace of friendship's tide.

Moments shared, both big and small,
Every memory, a cherished call.
In gentle words, we find that peace,
A bond unbroken, a sweet release.

Through sorrows deep and joys so bright,
You are my lantern, my guiding light.
With every tear, a steady hand,
In this journey, together we stand.

As seasons change and years go by,
Our roots grow deeper, reaching high.
In every heartbeat, laughter rings,
In friendship true, our spirit sings.

So let's embrace this path we tread,
With open hearts, no fear or dread.
In every moment, let love thrive,
In the embrace of friendship, we're alive.

A Circle of Life

In the dawn of day, life begins,
With whispered hopes on the breeze's wings.
Every sunrise tells a tale,
Of joy and struggle, the heart's trail.

In blooming flowers, stories unfold,
Of love and laughter, brave and bold.
Through laughter's echo, through tears we grow,
In nature's arms, we come to know.

The tides of time, they ebb and flow,
Carving paths in earth below.
Each moment a circle, vast and wide,
In every heartbeat, the world abides.

From cradle to dusk, we dance our song,
In the circle of life, where we belong.
With every ending, a brand new start,
Embracing all with an open heart.

So let us cherish this sacred thread,
In every silence, in words unsaid.
For in this journey, whatever strife,
We weave together the circle of life.

Currents of Encouragement

In the flow of gentle streams,
We find strength in silver gleams.
Wash away your doubt and fear,
Let the tides of hope draw near.

Each wave brings a fresh new start,
A whisper to the weary heart.
Feel the rhythm, trust the ride,
Faith will always be your guide.

As the current pulls you along,
Let your spirit sing its song.
Every ripple holds a cheer,
In the waters, love is here.

Embrace the change, it's in the flow,
Take the leap, and let it show.
With every splash, your worries cease,
In the current, find your peace.

So sail forth on waves so bright,
Let the currents bring you light.
Together, we will brave the seas,
In this journey, find your ease.

A Palette of Hope

With colors bold, we paint the sky,
Each hue a dream that dares to fly.
Brush strokes of joy in every shade,
A canvas bright where doubts do fade.

A splash of courage, a dash of grace,
In every corner, hope finds its place.
From dawn's soft blush to evening's glow,
A vibrant world awaits to show.

Mix in the laughter, stir in the cheer,
Let the vibrant colors draw you near.
For life's true art is ever bright,
In every shadow shines a light.

A palette filled with dreams untold,
Painted with warmth as hearts unfold.
With every layer, fears depart,
Creating visions, a work of heart.

So take the brush and dare to play,
In this gallery, find your way.
For hope is painted loud and clear,
A masterpiece that draws us near.

Seeds of Encouragement

Tiny seeds beneath the soil,
Hold the promise of new toil.
In stillness, they await the rain,
For growth comes softly from the pain.

Each gentle touch, each careful hand,
Nurtures life in this sacred land.
With patience springs each new delight,
From darkened earth, our dreams take flight.

In every bloom, a story's told,
Of courage bright and hearts so bold.
The roots spread wide, they intertwine,
In shared support, our spirits shine.

As seasons change, we learn to trust,
In every trial, rise we must.
For every seed holds hidden might,
A future filled with endless light.

So plant your hopes in fertile ground,
Let love and kindness be unbound.
For every blossom, bright and free,
Is the beauty of what's meant to be.

Wings of Warmth

With gentle beats that fill the air,
Wings of warmth float everywhere.
Embracing all with sweet caress,
A touch of love, a soft finesse.

When hearts are heavy, skies are gray,
Let these wings guide the way.
Through storms and trials, they will soar,
Whispering hope that opens doors.

A feather's light, a radiant glow,
This warmth within will help you grow.
In every flutter, a promise made,
To lift your spirit, never fade.

So feel the breeze that lifts your dreams,
As sunlight dances on the streams.
With every flap, you rise anew,
In warmth and light, you'll find what's true.

Embrace the winds that gently blow,
Let your heart take flight and flow.
For with each gust, you'll surely find,
Wings of warmth, forever kind.

Tides of Understanding

In the depths where whispers flow,
Currents pull, and insights grow.
Each wave brings a story near,
Washing doubts, embracing fear.

From shores of hope, we venture wide,
Navigating truth with gentle guide.
Together, we'll chart the unknown,
With every tide, our minds have grown.

As moonlight dances on the sea,
Awakening wonders within me.
We find our way through ebb and swell,
In this vast ocean, all is well.

The compass of our hearts aligned,
Through trials faced, our souls entwined.
With every crest, we learn, we thrive,
In currents deep, we feel alive.

Tides of understanding rise and fall,
Uniting us, embracing all.
In every wave, a voice, a call,
Together, we shall never stall.

Echoes of Empathy

In the silence, soft sounds play,
Whispers of care, leading the way.
Hearts attuned to pain and joy,
Compassion's thread, our shared alloy.

Through valleys low and mountains high,
We carry burdens, not shy to try.
With every step, we send the light,
Echoes of love will guide our sight.

Together we rise, together we fall,
Responding softly to each call.
Bridging the gaps, we stand as one,
In empathy's light, shadows undone.

With tender hands, reach out to all,
In every moment, big or small.
Let kindness reign as we explore,
Echoes of empathy, forevermore.

From hearts connected, a symphony grows,
In this melody, the spirit flows.
Together we find, in every way,
Echoes of empathy guide our stay.

Gentle Echoes

In the stillness, voices blend,
Whispers soft, to hearts extend.
A breeze that carries every thought,
Gentle echoes, love is taught.

In quiet corners where we meet,
Harmony makes our lives complete.
Each sound a thread that binds us tight,
Filling days and warming nights.

Through laughter's joy and sorrow's shade,
The echoes of our kindness made.
With every heartbeat, every sigh,
We share the truth, we dare to fly.

In the tapestry of time we weave,
Gentle echoes help us believe.
In every word, in every tone,
Together, we are never alone.

In moments fleeting, yet profound,
Gentle echoes all around.
They linger softly, touch the soul,
In unity, we feel whole.

Bonds Beyond Borders

Across the lands, beyond the seas,
A web of love carried by the breeze.
Cultures mingling, hearts embrace,
Bonds beyond borders, time and space.

With every step on foreign ground,
Familiar smiles begin to abound.
Laughter echoes, joy ignites,
In shared stories, our hope unites.

In diversity, strength is found,
Through kindness, we break new ground.
Hand in hand, we strive to build,
A world where all hearts are filled.

Language may differ, yet we share,
Dreams and visions, a world so rare.
Through open hearts, we'll find our way,
Bonds beyond borders lead the day.

Let love be our guiding star,
No matter where, no matter how far.
Together we rise, not torn apart,
Bonds beyond borders, the human heart.

Bridges Built with Kindness

In a world where shadows play,
Friendship lights the way.
We build our bridges strong and wide,
With every smile, we stand with pride.

A gentle word, a helping hand,
Together, we make a stand.
Hearts connect, both near and far,
Kindness shines, our guiding star.

Through storms and trials, we will stand,
With love and hope, our hearts expand.
Each act of care a steady beam,
Creating bonds, a vibrant dream.

In laughter shared and sorrows met,
A tapestry that we won't forget.
Bridges built with love and grace,
In every heart, a sacred space.

So let us stand, united, free,
With kindness as our legacy.
Together we'll rise, hand in hand,
With every kindness, a stronger land.

Illuminated Paths

Beneath the stars, our paths unfold,
In shadows cast, our dreams are bold.
We walk the trails of hope and light,
Guided gently through the night.

With every step, the way is clear,
Illuminated by those we hold dear.
The whispers of love, a soft embrace,
Filling our hearts, time can't erase.

In every corner, warmth we find,
As laughter dances, hearts entwined.
The road may bend, but we are strong,
Together we will sing our song.

Through darkened nights and stormy days,
We light the world in countless ways.
In unity, our spirits soar,
Illuminated paths forevermore.

So let us walk, our hearts ablaze,
Creating joy in endless maze.
With every step, together we rise,
Illuminated by love's skies.

Hands That Hold

Softly clasped, two hands entwined,
In gentle strength, our hearts aligned.
Through trials faced and joys we share,
Together, love, we learn to care.

With every touch, a promise made,
In darkest nights, a light displayed.
Through storms of life, we hold on tight,
In every moment, love's pure light.

Each hand that holds brings comfort near,
In silence shared, we conquer fear.
With fragile bonds, we build our trust,
In each embrace, we find what's just.

So lift your hands, let kindness flow,
In every heart, let love bestow.
For hands that hold, like roots of trees,
Can weather storms and dance with ease.

Together we rise, together we stand,
With grateful hearts, and open hands.
For every squeeze and loving hold,
Is warmth that can never grow old.

A Tapestry of Care

In threads of love, our stories weave,
A tapestry that we believe.
With every color, every hue,
We stitch a world that feels anew.

With kindness sewn in every seam,
A fabric rich with hopes and dreams.
We share our laughter, we share our tears,
And find our strength through all the years.

Each moment shared, every glance,
Creates a bond, a sacred dance.
In quiet spaces, we find our place,
A tapestry of love and grace.

Through trials faced and joys we find,
We build our world with hearts aligned.
In every stitch, a story told,
A tapestry of warmth, of gold.

So let us weave with threads so fine,
In every heart, our lives entwined.
Together we create and share,
A beautiful, resilient tapestry of care.

Lighthouses of Love

In the storm, you stand strong,
A beacon, guiding me along.
Through the fog, you shine bright,
Lighthouses of love, my guiding light.

With every wave that crashes near,
You calm my heart, you quell my fear.
Your warmth, a shelter from the cold,
In your embrace, my heart unfolds.

The night may try to steal our way,
But your light will never sway.
In the distance, I can see,
Lighthouses of love, forever free.

As ships seek harbor from the sea,
Your love is the anchor that grounds me.
Through rocky paths and tempest skies,
I find my home in your wise eyes.

So let the winds howl and the rain pour,
In your love, I'll always soar.
For no distance can ever part,
The lighthouses of love in my heart.

The Glow of Companionship

In quiet moments, side by side,
We share a world where dreams abide.
A gentle laugh, a knowing glance,
In the glow of companionship, we dance.

Through life's hustle, hand in hand,
Together we form a stronger band.
In every cheer, in every sigh,
Our spirits lift, as we fly high.

When shadows fall and troubles loom,
The glow of you dispels the gloom.
In every challenge, we face as one,
Together we rise, together we run.

Your presence warms the coldest nights,
In your company, the world feels right.
Two souls entwined, a bright array,
In the glow of companionship, we stay.

So here's to us, forever true,
In laughter, tears, and skies so blue.
With every day that comes to pass,
Our bond will shine, as bright as glass.

Melodies of Support

In silence, I hear your gentle tune,
A melody soft, beneath the moon.
You lift my heart with every note,
In the melodies of support, we float.

Through trials faced and paths unclear,
Your harmony whispers, always near.
In every rise, in every fall,
You are the music that fills it all.

With strings that weave our stories tight,
You are the rhythm in my fight.
In moments bleak, your song remains,
Melodies of support in countless refrains.

In laughter shared and tears we've shed,
Your voice, a comfort, where dreams are bred.
Together we create a symphony,
In the melodies of support, we are free.

So let the world around us change,
In our music, life feels strange.
For together, we'll write every line,
In the melodies of support, we intertwine.

The Heart's Embrace

In the quiet, I feel your beat,
A rhythm that makes my heart complete.
With every smile and tender trace,
I find my home in the heart's embrace.

Through challenges faced, we stand tall,
Your warmth is my shelter, my all.
In every tear and laughter's grace,
I find my peace in your heart's embrace.

Time may test, but love remains,
Through bittersweet and joyful gains.
We dance through storms, no wrong or place,
In the haven of the heart's embrace.

As seasons change and moments fly,
You are my anchor, the reason why.
With every step, in light or space,
I cherish the gift of the heart's embrace.

So here I stand, and here I stay,
In your arms, I've found my way.
For in this journey, my soul finds trace,
Forever woven in the heart's embrace.

Sanctuary of Supporters

In shadows deep where whispers dwell,
Kind hearts gather, a sacred shell.
With arms outstretched and voices raised,
They forge a bond that never fades.

Through storms of doubt, they lift us high,
Each gentle cheer, a sweet reply.
In times of need, they're never far,
A beacon bright, our guiding star.

With every tear, they share the pain,
Transforming loss to love's refrain.
In unity, they stand so tall,
A fortress strong, a safety wall.

Their laughter rings like joyful chimes,
Creating warmth in coldest climes.
A tapestry of hearts entwined,
In every soul, their strength combined.

In this sanctuary, hope ignites,
With every word, the spirit lights.
Together, in this hallowed space,
Supporters find their rightful place.

A Chorus of Champions

In fields aglow, where dreams take flight,
Champions gather, bold and bright.
With voices strong, they raise their song,
Together, where all hearts belong.

Each note a testament, fierce and clear,
Echoes of triumph, drawing near.
Through trials fierce, they find their way,
In unity, they seize the day.

With every step, their spirits soar,
A mighty band who yearn for more.
Together, they break every chain,
Resilience born from joy and pain.

In every heart, a fire burns,
With fervor strong, the passion churns.
They celebrate each small success,
In this great chorus, none are less.

With hands held high, they raise the stakes,
A brotherhood that never shakes.
In harmony, their voices blend,
A chorus where all hearts transcend.

Precious Parallels

In mirrored paths, we find our way,
Two souls aligned come what may.
With shared ambitions, dreams collide,
In tandem steps, we walk with pride.

Through trials faced, we learn to grow,
In every laugh, in every woe.
Together, we chart the unknown,
In precious parallels, we've grown.

Each twist and turn, a tale to tell,
In silent whispers, we do swell.
The strength of one makes two arise,
Our futures bright, a shared sunrise.

In moments hushed, our hearts ignite,
Illuminated by shared light.
In courage born, we blaze a trail,
In tandem, we will never fail.

As seasons change, we shift and sway,
In harmony, we find our way.
With every heartbeat, side by side,
In precious parallels, we abide.

Threads of Together

In woven strands, our lives entwine,
A tapestry where hearts align.
With every thread, a story spins,
In unity, our journey begins.

Each color vibrant, each pattern bright,
Together forging through day and night.
In laughter shared and burdens borne,
The fabric of love is gently worn.

With every stitch, new dreams emerge,
In harmony, our spirits surge.
A quilt of memories, warm and true,
In threads of together, we renew.

In trials faced, we are the seam,
Holding tight through every dream.
With every knot and every loop,
We build a bond that will not stoop.

In tangled paths where doubts may lie,
Together we reach for the sky.
With threads of together, we find grace,
In love's embrace, our cherished space.

Reflections of Solidarity

In times of strife, we stand as one,
Our voices join, a steady drum.
Together we face the raging tide,
In every heart, hope will abide.

Through storms that shake the world outside,
We find our strength, our spirits tied.
In laughter shared, in tears we share,
A bond is born, a love laid bare.

With every step, we lift each other,
In unity, we find our mother.
For every battle fought in vain,
Together we rise, transform the pain.

We weave a tapestry of trust,
A fortress built, it's strong and just.
In every face, a story found,
In solidarity, we are bound.

Let every heartbeat echo loud,
A call for peace, we stand unbowed.
Through every struggle, hand in hand,
We'll carve a path, we'll take a stand.

Passages of Grace

Each step a dance, a gentle glide,
Through fields of dreams, we choose to ride.
In whispered moments, we find our peace,
A song of joy, our hearts release.

The sun breaks through, a golden beam,
Awakening hopes, igniting dreams.
In simple acts of love and care,
We weave a world that's rich and rare.

Through trials faced, we learn to grow,
In shadows long, a soft light glows.
With every breath, we rise anew,
In passages of grace, we'll renew.

The winds will carry our laughter high,
As we embrace the open sky.
With open hearts, we take the leap,
In every moment, promises we keep.

And when we stumble, when we fall,
We rise together, standing tall.
For in each journey, love will place,
A mark divine, in passages of grace.

Lanterns in the Dark

When shadows loom and fears arise,
We light the way with hopeful eyes.
A flicker here, a glow so bright,
Together we find our guiding light.

In every heart, a lantern waits,
To spark the fire, to open gates.
With every soul, a story told,
In darkness deep, our dreams unfold.

Through tangled paths and winding roads,
We carry hope, we lift the loads.
For every journey taken near,
Our lanterns shine, dispelling fear.

A flickering flame, a pulse of trust,
In bonds we share, we must, we must.
For in the dark, we find our way,
With lanterns bright, we seize the day.

So hold your light, don't let it fade,
In unity, we're never afraid.
Together, we'll banish every spark,
And walk as one, through shadows dark.

Connections that Nurture

In every glance, a story brews,
Connections made, hearts warm with hues.
Through laughter shared and tears alike,
We build the bridges, hearts ignite.

With gentle words, we cultivate,
A garden rich, a bond innate.
In quiet moments, love will grow,
Through every challenge, together we flow.

The roots we plant, they stretch so deep,
A treasure trove for us to keep.
In every hug, in every smile,
Connections nurture, we walk each mile.

Through seasons change, through dusk and dawn,
We find our way, our love reborn.
For in the dance of life we partake,
These connections made, we will not break.

A tapestry woven, threads entwine,
In every heart, a love divine.
Together, we rise, our spirits soar,
In connections that nurture, forevermore.

Colors of Caring

In hues of kindness, hearts unite,
A tapestry woven, pure and bright.
Each thread a gesture, warm and true,
Colors of caring, in all we do.

Gentle greens of empathy show,
Soft blues of peace in every glow.
The reds of passion, fierce and strong,
Together we flourish, where we belong.

Golden rays of laughter ignite,
Bringing warmth in the darkest night.
Through every moment, every hour,
Caring bonds bloom, a vibrant flower.

In the palette of life, we blend,
Every shadow, a chance to mend.
Colors of caring, bright and vast,
Together we'll make each moment last.

Hand in hand, we paint the sky,
With strokes of hope that never die.
In colors of caring, we find our way,
A masterpiece born with each new day.

Pathways of Partnership

Two hearts wandering, side by side,
On pathways where dreams do abide.
With every step in trust we tread,
Hand in hand, by love we're led.

The roads may twist, the journey wide,
In harmony, we'll ever glide.
Through valleys low and mountains high,
Partnership's wings allow us to fly.

In moments shared, our spirits blend,
Through laughter and tears, together we mend.
A compass of love, we follow true,
In every path, it's me and you.

When storms arise and shadows loom,
Our bond shines bright, dispelling gloom.
With every heartbeat, we navigate,
Partnership's strength, we celebrate.

As seasons change and time rolls on,
Together we rise at each new dawn.
Pathways of partnership, forevermore,
In unity, we soar and explore.

Waves of Wellness

Gentle tides bring peace to shores,
Each wave a whisper, love restores.
In the rhythm of life we flow,
Waves of wellness, soft and slow.

With every crash, we learn to heal,
Embracing the moments that life reveals.
The sun sets low, yet hope remains,
In waves of wellness, joy regains.

As currents shift and seas may roar,
We stand together, hearts explore.
In tranquil waters, we find our place,
Waves of wellness, a warm embrace.

Each ripple spreads the love we feel,
A tide of kindness, ever real.
In harmony, we rise and dive,
In waves of wellness, we come alive.

Together we surf on dreams so bright,
Navigating through day and night.
In every splash, a story's spun,
Waves of wellness, our journey's begun.

Illuminated Journeys

With lanterns lit, we cross the night,
In search of wisdom, love, and light.
Each step reveals a path unclear,
Illuminated journeys, drawing near.

The stars above guide our way,
A map of dreams in shades of gray.
With courage deep, we face the unknown,
Together we journey, never alone.

In every shadow, a lesson lies,
The sparkle of hope, where spirit flies.
Through trials faced, our hearts align,
Illuminated journeys, truly divine.

We gather strength in shared embrace,
In every moment, finding grace.
With every story, a flame ignites,
Illuminated journeys, our hearts take flight.

As we explore this wondrous land,
Side by side, we understand.
In the glow of love, we find our way,
Illuminated journeys guide our day.

Veils of Protection

Soft whispers cloak the soul,
In shadows where secrets dwell,
A shelter built from pure intention,
Where fears are quelled, and hope can swell.

Woven threads of love surround,
Each layer shields from bitter pain,
Resilient shields we hold so dear,
Through storms we stand, we shall remain.

The heart encased in gentle care,
A fortress held by trust's embrace,
With every breath, a prayer sent high,
We find our strength in this safe space.

Guided by the stars above,
Each heartbeat echoes through the night,
In veils of warmth, we find our path,
Together we embrace the light.

Forever bound by sacred ties,
We dance beneath the moonlit skies,
In veils of protection, love will bloom,
Our spirits rise, dispelling gloom.

Aligning Hearts

In silence where two souls converge,
A harmony begins to sing,
Like melodies that softly merge,
The warmth of love ignites its ring.

Gentle whispers in the night,
Each heartbeat syncs, a sweet refrain,
Through tangled paths, we find our light,
An echo strong that holds no chains.

Like stars that point the way ahead,
Our dreams align like constellations,
In every glance, our truths are said,
Crafting stories, fueling passions.

Together we draw circles wide,
Creating spaces rich and free,
In unity, we gently glide,
Finding strength in harmony.

Aligning hearts, our spirits rise,
In unison, we boldly stand,
With open arms to grasp the skies,
The universe reveals its plan.

The Warmth of Presence

In moments sweet, our laughter weaves,
A blanket stitched with threads of grace,
Each heartbeat holds the light it leaves,
   A warmth in time, a soft embrace.

Through fleeting days, your smile remains,
  A touch that soothes the restless mind,
    In stillness, love softly sustains,
  A refuge where our hearts can bind.

Like sunlight breaking through the haze,
   Your presence ignites quiet fires,
  With every glance, we drift in rays,
A dance of dreams, where hope inspires.

  The warmth of presence fills the air,
  With words unspoken, we can feel,
   In every moment, pure and rare,
    Unraveling what's truly real.

   In simple joys, our spirits soar,
   As love envelops every scene,
   In warmth we find forevermore,
    A bond unbroken and serene.

Mosaics of Motivation

In fragments bright, our dreams reside,
Each piece a jewel, shining clear,
Together they create the guide,
A masterpiece we hold so dear.

With every step, we rise and strive,
We weave our stories filled with spark,
Through trials faced, we learn to thrive,
With faith ignited in the dark.

Mosaics formed from hopes and schemes,
Each shard reflects a part of fate,
In unity, we chase our dreams,
Creating paths that resonate.

With colors bold, we paint our lives,
A tapestry of heart and soul,
Through every challenge, love survives,
Together we emerge as whole.

Mosaics of motivation rise,
In visions shared, we find our reign,
Each piece a spark that never dies,
In this grand work, our hearts remain.

Radiant Ripples of Assistance

In quiet moments, kindness flows,
A gentle touch, where compassion grows.
Hearts unite, a bond we share,
In radiant ripples, love fills the air.

Hands extended, we lift each other,
Facing storms, we stand together.
Light the path for those in need,
With every act, we plant a seed.

Bridges built with words so kind,
Inshared struggles, hope we find.
Through the dark, a guiding light,
In our hearts, we spark the night.

Embrace the strength in unity,
In every tear, a glimpse of beauty.
Together, we can rise above,
In every ripple, we weave our love.

So let us stand with open arms,
Where honesty and grace disarm.
With open hearts, we will ignite,
The radiant ripples, shining bright.

Shades of Solace

Underneath the twilight sky,
In quiet whispers, dreams fly high.
Each moment shared, a gentle blend,
In shades of solace, hearts transcend.

A canvas painted with soft hues,
In shadows cast, we find our muse.
Comfort found in tender care,
In every glance, there's beauty rare.

With open arms, we share the weight,
Hearts entwined, we navigate fate.
Through life's maze, together roam,
In shades of solace, we find home.

A melody of peace we sing,
In every challenge, hope takes wing.
Through the storms, our spirits soar,
In unity, we open the door.

So let us cherish each calm night,
In every shadow, find the light.
With gentle strength, we will embrace,
The shades of solace in this place.

Tapestry of Trust

Threads of honesty, woven tight,
In every heart, a guiding light.
Together stitched through joy and pain,
In the tapestry of trust, we gain.

Colors blend in vibrant hues,
In shared stories, we can't lose.
With every knot, a promise made,
Through trials faced, we won't fade.

Each moment shared, a thread so fine,
In every smile, our lives entwine.
With open hearts, we weave anew,
A tapestry of trust so true.

In every tear, a strength revealed,
Through tender bonds, our fates are sealed.
With every laugh, our spirits fly,
In this fabric, we touch the sky.

So let us cherish every seam,
In this work of love, forever dream.
With faith in hand, we will engage,
The tapestry of trust we stage.

Harmonies of Hope

In the silence, whispers ring,
A melody of hope takes wing.
Through every trial, we stand tall,
In harmonies of hope, we learn to call.

With open arms, we gather near,
In every laugh, we conquer fear.
Together, crafting dreams anew,
In this symphony, hearts stay true.

With every note, we rise and blend,
In the music, love shall mend.
Through shadows deep, a light does gleam,
In harmonies of hope, we dream.

So let us sing with joyful hearts,
In every echo, the spirit starts.
Together strong, we will inspire,
In this chorus, ignite the fire.

With each refrain, a bond we share,
In unity, we breathe the air.
With hope as guide, we'll always cope,
In every sound, discover hope.

Uniting Forces

In the heart of struggle, we take a stand,
Hand in hand, we form a band.
Together we rise, together we fall,
A united power, we heed the call.

Voices join in harmony's tune,
Underneath the sun, and beneath the moon.
Differences set aside, aligned we strive,
In the dance of hope, we come alive.

Through challenge and doubt, we push on through,
In the light of courage, we find the true.
The weight of the world, we share as one,
With each step forward, we've only begun.

Every journey starts with a single thread,
A tapestry woven, where all are fed.
In this grand embrace, no place for hate,
Together, we're stronger, together, we're great.

With hope as our guide, we forge ahead,
Through storms and shadows, we're never misled.
In the book of unity, we write our page,
A tale of resilience, a brand new stage.

The Safety Net

In the arms of trust, we find our place,
A gentle embrace, a warm, safe space.
When storms are fierce, and shadows loom,
In our circle of care, we banish gloom.

We lift each other, when burdens are high,
With words of comfort, we help spirits fly.
Through whispers of hope, we weave our thread,
A safety net spun, where none are misled.

With kindness as guide, we journey as one,
Through trials and troubles, we seize the sun.
In laughter and tears, we share the load,
A bridge of connection, on this weary road.

Together, we rise, from ashes and dust,
In the heart of our bond, we find the trust.
An anchor in chaos, a beacon bright,
In the tapestry of life, we become the light.

The safety net holds, through thick and thin,
In the dance of life, we spin and we grin.
With every heartbeat, we build and repair,
A circle unbroken, with love in the air.

Fostering Unity

In the garden of souls, we plant the seeds,
Of compassion and kindness, fulfilling our needs.
With gentle hands, we nurture and grow,
A bond of true friendship, we love and we show.

Diverse are our voices, but one is our goal,
Creating a space where all feel whole.
Through laughter and tears, we share our plight,
In the tapestry woven, we find the light.

Together we strive, on this path we tread,
With open hearts, there's nothing to dread.
In moments of silence, our spirits unite,
A symphony of purpose, shining so bright.

With every small gesture, like droplets of rain,
We foster a unity, through joy and pain.
In the warmth of our bond, we flourish and thrive,
In the circle of love, we feel so alive.

So let us embrace, each color and sound,
In this vibrant world, let unity abound.
With arms wide open, we welcome the new,
Together as one, we'll always pull through.

A Garden of Guidance

In a garden of wisdom, we plant our dreams,
With roots intertwined, bursting at the seams.
The flowers of knowledge bloom all around,
In the light of understanding, true growth is found.

With gentle hands, we tend to each sprout,
Watering hopes through shadows of doubt.
In the sun's warm embrace, mentors arise,
Sprinkling their insights beneath endless skies.

The seasons will change, but love will remain,
In this sanctuary, we either smile or sustain.
Through the storms of life, we journey and learn,
In the garden of guidance, our spirits will burn.

We share what we've learned, we nurture and grow,
In the face of adversity, our courage will show.
With patience and care, our roots intertwine,
In the beauty of growth, our futures align.

Hand in hand, we tend to our space,
With gratitude, kindness, and warmth we embrace.
In this garden of guidance, we each play a part,
Cultivating a haven that nurtures the heart.

Bridges Built on Compassion

In the heart where kindness flows,
We build bridges, wide and close.
Each smile exchanged, each hand held tight,
Creates a path from dark to light.

No fear can stand where love's embraced,
In compassion's warmth, all hearts can race.
Together we rise, united in grace,
With every step, our fears we face.

For every tear that gently falls,
A bridge emerges, love calls.
In every struggle, we find a way,
Compassion's beacon, brightens the day.

We paint the world with hues of care,
Tears of joy and pain we share.
With open hearts and minds we meet,
In this harmony, life is sweet.

So come together, hand in hand,
As our spirits take a stand.
For bridges built on love will last,
A future bright, our shadows cast.

Currents of Coexistence

In the river where we flow,
Currents blend, and harmony grows.
Different streams, yet one we rise,
An ocean where the spirit flies.

With every wave that touches shore,
We find the strength to seek for more.
Together, though we swim apart,
In unity, we find our heart.

Let not the tide pull us away,
For in our depths, there's light to sway.
Embracing differences with grace,
In every angle, love we trace.

From distant lands, our voices call,
In the dance of life, we're one and all.
Currents swirl, yet peace we cultivate,
In coexistence, we elevate.

Through every storm, we learn to sail,
On unity, we'll never fail.
Together we rise, from sea to sea,
In currents of love, we find the key.

Seeds of Encouragement

In the garden where dreams take flight,
We plant the seeds, with hope in sight.
With every word, we water ground,
In nurturing, our strength we've found.

Encouragement is sunlight's ray,
That helps the fragile shoot to sway.
In shadows deep or skies so wide,
With steadfast love, we will abide.

Each seed we sow, a promise dear,
To hold each other close and near.
Through storms and winds, we stand as one,
As flowers bloom, our fears undone.

In every heart, a garden grows,
With tender care, the beauty shows.
We cultivate each soul we meet,
In every struggle, rise to greet.

For in the soil of time and trust,
We find our strength, we know we must.
As seasons change, we thrive and grow,
In seeds of hope, our love will flow.

Chords of Connection

In the melody of life we sing,
Chords of hope, together bring.
Each note a bond that ties us tight,
Harmonies that fill the night.

From different strings, with voices clear,
We weave a song that all can hear.
In every rhythm, joy resounds,
Connection found in the hearts' bounds.

With gentle strums, we break the mold,
In every tale, a truth unfolds.
Together, we create a score,
In chords of love, we're evermore.

In unison, we rise to dance,
Each step a chance, a new romance.
As melodies intertwine so sweet,
The music of life, a wondrous feat.

So let the orchestra play on strong,
In every heart, we all belong.
For in this concert, life's direction,
Together we find chords of connection.

Milton Keynes UK
Ingram Content Group UK Ltd.
UKHW022143111124
451073UK00007B/167

9 789916 866412